For Girls Who Become Women

Jessica Alyse Hamilton

To my sister friends,

Who showed me strength,

who showed me the beauty in womanhood and myself.

To my sister by kin,

Who has read every version of this book before the story left my pen,

who hasn't left my side since I entered this world.

To my Mommy and Daddy,

Who gave life to this girl,

who believed in me enough to support anything I have ever dreamt of being,

Who paid for me to think freely -

I love you.

The Introduction

I wrote this book throughout the passing of many seasons.

Some days I was strong,

Some days I questioned my existence.

All in all I survived, and this is a testament of the strength of a heart;

and its ability to break and repair again - all in the same lifetime.

I spent my lifetime,

waiting for reassurance,

ignoring embedded torment,

The things that made me settle for less.

After writing this- never again.

I wish you that same freedom.

Here, take this - I got it for you |

There once was a girl,

Brave enough to love

But not yet brave enough to love herself

She went through hell,

To prove that she'd do anything

Lost her sanity,

exchanged it for being his everything

Exchanged *herself t*o prove that she could sacrifice.

What becomes of a girl

Who put her worth

in hands not made for holding

Who solely defines being hopeless,

As a life without being loved.

Who would rather cry defeat

than attempt to see,

who she was meant to be

without him.

This growth was not easy

But it brought out the deepest,

Parts of my being

Showed me beauty,

that I never gave myself credit for.

God has a way of teaching lessons, without our consent
-

For Girls Who Become Women

I am grateful.

Your Fire |

Your fire promised me warmth,

then scorched my dignity at first touch.

Made me believe that I am better off freezing,

than believing

you were ever my comfort.

Up and Down |

I am your helium balloon you picked up from the
circus.

You inflate and deflate me at your leisure.

On days you feel like seeing me fly,

you fill me up with promise.

Others you take the air from me,

watch me

cascade from sky to floor

When you show me you'll never change.

I am starting to feel ashamed

of how my shape is morphed by you

How everything you do

effects my composition.

You are the perfect magician,

Can freeze me in time

Convince me that I

Am flying without wings

Almost feel free

until you tug on that string

Always say that one thing,

that makes me believe in you again.

The Markings of the Discarded |

My first real heartbreak left me unidentified.

Crawling under sheets

To find missing pieces of me,

Knowing he scattered them frivolously

Thinking it'd be best to search everywhere.

There is a pain that resonates with those who have been discarded,

indents in our palms

from holding on to a fighting,

heart that no longer wanted to be ours.

There are trails,

from tear ducts to toes

letting the water heal the places he used to touch,

thinking if you cried enough

he'd find his way back home.

There is the home

that never feels like home

because his voice echoes in the walls,

we can distinctly recall when he said he'd never leave.

So how did we get here?

Women who have loved

as if they trusted nothing and no one else

can find each other on dirt roads,

trying to retrace their steps.

Asking strangers to point out where

we were not enough,

and if they can lead us back so that we can try again.

We stand unbalanced,

as if grief knocked us off our feet

as if the sight of him will bring us to our knees

as if we would fall again if he'd catch us.

There are markings on lovers

who have loved others

who thought our best wasn't enough.

So are we even enough,

is marked on everything we do.

I spent a lifetime building the me,

That you gave away for free

Empty,

would be an understatement.

The Living Color |

He left her womb an empty room.

No one cried but the woman it belonged to.

No tears shed from the man she used to call friend,

that helped her decorate it all.

He never wondered where the pretty things went,

Never thought to ask her did she miss them.

Never wondered what life could have been,

if they kept it all.

Some nights I reach for the paintings on the wall,

Reach for the baby dolls that would have been perfect
for a girl or boy

Reach for the only thing I thought,

would love me back without conditions.

Without intentions,

because decor is grateful for just existing

Never hear it whispering,

it would rather be somewhere else -

Can't,

fall in love with someone else

Can't,

belong to someone else

Can't leave you with nothing.

I reach and gather dust,

Regrets of youth, unprepared and not stable enough

For Girls Who Become Women

Regrets of thinking there was enough love -

to do right by you.

I feel it in the quiet, I hear it in the silence

I will never forget this womb was once violet

I relive the day it was painted blue,

like it was yesterday

Could vividly replay the day,

 the colors were stripped away -

I cry for you sometimes.

Jaded, She has Faded.|

You think you're over something until you realize you can't stop typing. You think the lesson is over, go educate the masses - but I can go on for days about the demise of my faith in people. That witnessing an ex-lover become ex-human has made me the same way. I can attest to feeling bionic because human hurts. I can say that trust is no longer in my vocabulary.

This is the phase of my growth that requires me to rid myself of resentments. The part when I forgive you for not knowing better, or caring less if you did. This is the part that I tell every woman that a man does not define you, you are woman alone.

I can still hear lies. I can still feel loss. Only it is no longer shaped like you. You are no longer the picture I put up to the punching bag. I have traded you in.

Instead you made the world my picture, everything that was animated is now dull.

For Girls Who Become Women

I no longer live in color.

There are no walls between me and love after, there are
skyscrapers ascending from the depths of my heart.

I am in the phase of my growth where I take my power
back, and reclaim myself.

                                   But I need more time.

Hollow |

This heart is so hollow, that it will let you in

just because there's room enough -

But don't mistake this for real shelter.

You may hear I love you back when you say it first;

but it is only your own words,

bouncing off the walls

Soon enough you'll become familiar with the echo.

It's cold in here most nights,

some may even say frigid

but warm blood is only for the living

everything in this heart has lost its pulse.

For Girls Who Become Women

There was a raid in this cave quite some time ago

They swept it, of all things beautiful

Took the hope right off the walls.

So I'm so sorry if there are no pictures.

No welcome signs to make this feel like home.

Haven't prioritized decoration,

been too busy adjusting to life alone

Too busy searching this soul,

didn't have much time to make it pretty.

Wonder Girl |

I once believed that I had super powers.

That my vagina,

could morph the slightest interest into love

could transform the hardest rock into a warm touch,

Could make a romantic out of the jaded.

Now some say there's love and then there's lust.

But superheroes don't believe in boundaries

have no respect for distinctions.

Believe that everything they want and dream

is limitless

Have no interest in what things are in the present.

For Girls Who Become Women

See,

us heroes know these thighs mimic heaven,

might even teach you how to fly after we're finished -

Could show you a thing or two about imagination.

How to save the world,

How to love a girl,

How to be someone

who doesn't leave first thing in the morning.

I have a cool trick that provokes an I love you,

just working on how to use it

outside of the bedroom

I am still working out the kinks.

I once believed that I had superpowers

That even when I was invisible

you believed in me,

even when I was weak

you needed me,

even when I am an inch from hitting ground

you think that I am capable.

Think that I am able - to save the day.

I think that I,

am better when I see myself this way

I can fantasize all day,

about what it is like to not be human.

Because that would just make me stupid,

a foolish woman whose looseness

thinks it can pass for heroic.

I may not be wonder-woman

but I am a damn good poet,

which means I can make lost –

sound powerful.

Brown Sugar |

I tried replacing your touch.

It felt like nails on a chalkboard.

Felt like everything you do right,

done wrong

Feels like I am -

desperately filling voids.

I tried to replace you, and my laugh doesn't sound the same.

What I'd hope would be an escape

Is simply being face to face

With the fact that I still love you.

His arms feel like you left me,

like you promised you would come back.

Like my heart knows your fingerprints

like alarms started ringing;

 Fraud alert.

His touch feels like we tried and failed

It is painful being here,

Without you.

I am

Between a rock and a hard place

Being alone is a sad day

But being held wrong,

Is just a replay

Of my insecurities.

Just some Fools in Love |

To every girl who's been told that you would be
perfect, he's just not ready. Grab a tissue and sit next to
me. Join the club of almost doesn't count, the ones that
would wait right here until he is.

Welcome to lovers' anonymous- where our willingness
to settle disguises itself as patience, where our bleeding
hearts pass for bravery, where we cover all clocks.

See, we hold our meeting in the dark

so no one can see the scars,

we stare at hour glasses until they stop,

then we begin again.

We tell ourselves we're waiting for fate and epiphanies
to collide

That he just needs a little more time,

but our hair is beginning to thin.

Our wrinkles are more apparent,

our bones clicking like champagne flutes

We've ran out of things to do

We've shared our stories of how we always knew

that he was meant for us,

Watched these old carpets gather dust,

We wait for the front door to creak.

Sometimes we don't even speak,

The silence helps recall you in a daydream,

Helps remember what it feels like

to love you.

I am growing old here,

For Girls Who Become Women

Starting to run out of reasons to fade away here,

Haven't seen light in 226 days,

I could even forget your name

If it was not embedded in my waist,

If I didn't memorize the trace

of your fingertips on my skin.

I put a lifetime aside,

Called it "giving you some time"

But even that ran out.

It's time to grow some pride

Let this resentment of mine,

grow a spine

Enough to walk out that door.

Nothing left to be hopeful for,

Because the truth is; if you needed me

you'd be back by now.

Markings of the Discarded | II |

There are markings on lovers

who have recovered

from the storm of a broken heart.

Scarred chests from repairs,

remnants of being brave enough

to try to live again.

My ears don't hear the same as they used to,

turned bionic in search of the truth;

looks for the punchline in everything seemingly
sincere.

How is it fair,

that my damage is visible.

That there was a war

And the only proof it ever was

Is my resistance to the word love.

How I shake at the thought of intimacy.

How can you stand straight up?

Limbs moving as if losing us

didn't hit you unexpectedly.

Like,

you're in-tact without me.

Like,

our memories don't haunt your dreams.

Like,

you must not feel a thing.

For Girls Who Become Women

I thought you robot.

Metal.

Only something inhumane could not feel this pain,

could ignore this sting and just go about living.

But you are human.

                              You just didn't love me back.

| *T* |

Untangle my love from yours I've tried to,

Pick myself for once I need to,

I am tired of not knowing where I start.

Every time I reach to guard my heart

There is a hellish fight

of who needs to be protected more,

A straight up war

against self-preservation,

A question of who can best survive the damage,

Of who can best manage

without a beating heart.

I always say I'm stronger,

For Girls Who Become Women

Willingly play martyr

for the boy who would always pick himself-

when given the choice.

Self-sacrifice for a boy,

I know was never nurtured enough

Tell myself that wound is likely to bleed out faster

I have become a master

at putting you first.

At diving heart first,

At nursing my wounds with reused tissues

I've used to drain rivers I've cried out for you.

I am tired of being your fool,

Of knowing that my work

will always be perceived as donations

Never worth the compensation,

of loving me back.

I've spent years in training,

holding weights, practiced not breaking

Under your weight - from being your crutch

Practiced catching you before you fall.

Practiced, risking it all

Even practiced what I'd say if you ever said

Thank you.

For the girls who never received apologies or gratitude,
who became an unvalued tool, because you thought he
couldn't survive without you -

For Girls Who Become Women

Let him bleed,

Let him fall,

Let him lose it all,

Because at the end of it all

-

You're already proof that he can survive too,

Because you already survived it martyr.

Didn't you?

You're still alive |

There comes this fork in the road,

Just a straight up choice

Of whether you're going to keep breaking

Or toughen up.

I grew tired,

of being fragile.

RED.|

For all the things that you forgive,

ask yourself would he do the same.

Would he stay?

We plaster apologies on our walls and call ourselves martyrs.

Call ourselves Christ like.

Call ourselves Lovers.

For all the plastered apologies

Check the frames for cracks.

Because tears don't bond like super glue,

You may need to replace that.

We are not stronger for staying,

no less burnt for standing in fire,

no more hero for trying to save men

who don't see the fault in it all.

Get no medals for harboring repeat offenders.

What you call redemption is conscious repetition

Constant depending,

On our blind forgiveness,

our willingness to break.

I say,

We start a revolution.

Close our ears to the excuses,

That leave us half empty and ruined.

I say we flood the streets,

Let them know that we are no longer lambs but beasts

That the feeling of defeat - no longer suits us.

It is time for the rise of the Queens

I...*forgive you.*/

I hate you so much,

that I forgot that you were beautiful,

Forgot that I ever felt heaven in your touch.

Rage has a way of not remembering much,

Of clearing out what made me love you in the first place.

You are not all bad,

And I am not all broken.

In fact, all this pain comes from hoping

I was deserving

to be held by you for always.

I still miss the way,

You sound speechless when you say my name

For Girls Who Become Women

Can't think of a day that I'd ever hear it the same

after it left your lips

I still hear songs

that remind me,

We were more right than wrong

That there was a time that all you wanted to do was
learn me.

Unravel me -

You grew addicted to the feeling,

Never stopped spinning me,

Until I came undone.

I thought, you were getting to the hard stuff.

Stripping all this hard stuff,

of all the unnecessities.

But you got to the necessities -

and shed those too.

She can't breathe

Without those things.

Give them back,

I'll exchange them for anything,

Anything except forgiveness.

I tried forgiving you once,

                      - this is what it looked like.

For Girls Who Become Women

| ; my Janae |

I know too many women,

Who have revived themselves without assistance,

Who have redefined their existence -

to believe that I will die from this.

Shared the same womb as my sister-

Which means I came out fearless,

Which means I stand a chance,

at living again.

She is living again,

Reincarnated as a Queen

who now has the strength to believe

That she is meant to be here

That we may all shed some tears here,

but life's worth waiting out

to see what God has been watering for us.

That,

at times you may feel your soul ready to combust,

Close as hell to giving up

So hurt that you doubt your own mind.

May,

lose your balance in your sleep some nights

even weep some nights,

But you find that thing worth fighting for.

For Girls Who Become Women

That one thing that you adore-

And you grasp it for dear life.

She reached into pitch black

Came out with an inch of light

that saved her own life -

Loved herself twice as hard,

so that she could see mine

put heart ache aside -

because she knew I couldn't survive,

without her.

Who some named unworthy-

She named a lifeline

I will never feel a greater love in this lifetime-

I have been loved enough for lifetimes,

I will survive this.

If she did it I know I can,

I will never understand

What she chose to withstand

to be here for me.

So I will feel everything.

The ugly and the deep,

The pain and the suffering be brave enough to

Face it all.

Because she did it all,

I have never been more proud.

| *famished.* |

To all the hearts I burned while igniting my fire,

I apologize.

To all the figures I used as shadow from the truth,

this one's for you -

A lost woman can't lead you to the truth,

even if she means to -

Can't guide you to the light in her darkness.

I used your bodies for catharsis,

thought harboring hearts in my closet would make me

feel,

Full.

But every heart I ate sank down to my shoes,

only fed my blues,

did nothing for the building of

Me.

Felt like

Fine dining corpses,

pretty pointless

Because she never tasted a thing.

But,

Lies aren't lies when you're convinced that they're true,

So I meant that I was good for you

Just didn't know I couldn't see it through,

Didn't know that I was looking for the me, in you.

I rummaged through relationships

looking for safe places

looking for safe havens,

looking for identity.

So imagine my surprise

when I found your heart

on a search for mine,

Beating brave enough to love me

But not scholar enough to read the signs

Too blind to see that she says: empty.

I can't trust someone who's fond of broken,

Who doesn't know the difference

between silver dollars and tokens,

who can't see counterfeit in the daylight.

For Girls Who Become Women

So I tell myself,

This must be a farce.

You must see the scars

You must want to reopen wounds

just to hear me moan for you.

You must want me damaged.

So I project it,

get relentless,

Get ready to claim you fool

before you claim me worthy.

Say all you will do is hurt me,

convert me into someone

you'd rather know instead.

I bring you fire just to see what you make of it,

take all your shit and break it –

just to see if you can handle me at my worst.

Let the bad go first,

because she'll come out someday.

anyway

I need to know now if you'll walk away,

but who wouldn't escape flames,

to protect themselves.

I am tired of burning.

I hurt you, it's true.

But not because I meant to.

For Girls Who Become Women

I was waiting on God to take me to healing.

So for anyone I promised flights to

before I found my wings,

I am sorry that my name reminds you to lock up
valuable things,

That I remind you to guard your heart.

Sorry that I left dirty footprints all over your art,

sorry that I made a mess while passing through,

And while I know poetry isn't super glue

I hope your heart is mending,

that my truth helps you realize that the girl you knew
was bending,

Shape shifting, into someone brave enough to love
herself.

You couldn't have loved me any different,

Give you an A for effort and good intention.

I was just busy purging myself renewed.

Thank you,

for trying to be my food.

| *There are roots,*

To everything that hurt you.

Retrace them,

take your time

And learn yourself to healing. |

| *I dug and I found,* **you.**|

I heard my mom's life story at 24,

I curled up in a ball and cried for her.

Tears falling like ink on paper that never got to dry,

making a mess of everything that once was white.

Surprised that I ever villainized,

something so

resilient.

I cried for the times that I watched her shaking,

for the times that my heart was too busy breaking

to beat for two,

I think, had I been in your shoes I would not be here,

The type of pain you've seen would make it unfair

to expect much left for two daughters.

I am honored

and confused,

to have a lineage of women torn and bruised

of you being the first to choose,

to see what's on the other side of broken.

You were chosen -

To show us that repaired things are just as good as new,

If not even more valuable

That these cracks are called abstract in houses that
appreciate the truth

You are my roots.

And when I cry I hope to water the soil that was never
turned for you

Would dig up planted earth for you,

to show you that you are worth the work.

I never understood why you didn't know what you
were worth,

Why you'd always asked twice if we loved our
mommy.

I am sorry, that they never said it to you.

But for what it's worth

I think that you are worth,

Telling every ounce of truth I know for your
redemption -

Living every day with intention

to show you that God had a plan.

That you weren't buried in sand,

you were planted to make something beautiful.

Each time I blossom you smile, I now understand why;

I am truly a flower child.

| *God knows, I found you too.* |

I have always had my daddy's smile

And fragile heart

Gained his hands

And his slowness to reprimand,

The people that hurt him.

We share that flexibility,

We show when we try to people please

Show our common fragility,

When we get hurt in return.

Never give ourselves time to be imperfect,

Because someone else's broken

For Girls Who Become Women

Always triumphs over ours

Our scars,

are scratches

Compared to the damage,

We witness on those we love

Saying no,

Is something that comes from the depths of our souls

Only accessible

if we're already twice empty.

We've been twice emptied,

And still apologize after draining.

I never told you,

that I cried after you left

Took whiffs of your clothes and wept

Resented you for using your sense

And moving to safety.

You never abandoned me,

Saw you almost daily

Called me every second of every minute

But home felt dark without you in it

Couldn't help but to admit-

I felt like you taught me everything

but how to loosen a grip,

and when you finally did

For Girls Who Become Women

I dropped on the floor.

My heart couldn't endure,

the first time you chose yourself.

Dear Mommy, and Daddy.

I forgive you.

I love you.

I know you did your best.

The Markings of the Discarded | **III** |

She stands straight up.

As if the worst of luck

couldn't knock her off her feet.

She gleams.

As if daring you try,

As if getting up twice

is something she mastered along the way.

There are markings on women who've found
themselves along the way,

a distinct pride that resides,

in knowing of your craftiness.

that you can now make any mess, beautiful.

You become the artist your mother raised.

Throwing paint and brave enough together to make,

something magical.

You learn that the best art comes from things
unplanned.

You begin to understand,

that pain was sent to make a warrior out of you.

There is a world after heartache.

One that looks like everything you called mistakes

Lessons that made you great,

Reminders that you are durable.

I am standing when I never thought I'd walk again,

thought the loss of him -

would nail me to the ground.

For Girls Who Become Women

I have found,

the beauty in starting over.

I am loving myself,

when I thought I never knew her,

when I thought she only mattered in his arms.

I am a new masterpiece,

Draped in strength and calligraphy

Huge letters so that everyone can see -

that she knows that she's enough this time.

Outro

For Girls Who Become Women | *Mother, You're an Artist* |

Your mother teaches you what it is to become woman. Be it incorrect, absentee or broken- you mimic her until God interferes. Until God says that no one of flesh can teach you what it is to be whole, that woman was made in his likeness.

My mother is a survivor of incorrect teaching. A scholar amongst women who unintentionally gave her little to study, a jack of illegitimate trades. She used her hands and intentions and sculpted womanhood for our home, molded it together with often motherless and still wounded. Gave it everything that she had in the present, we named it Guidance.

While we admired it at first, saw it as the first piece of art in our hallways there were days where the light showed its' shortcomings. Where angles exposed the holes, she tried to pass for pattern when she simply didn't know what was supposed to go there.

She collected things throughout the day, tried to shove
them in at night. Hoped we wouldn't catch her
working, that we'd just wake up to a masterpiece; but
darkness and reference-less does little for perfection.

My sister and I became obsessive, looking for the flaws
before the beauty, began clashing over creative
differences; thought at times we'd rather have blank
than imperfect.

Mother.

I have grown to know

that it is a skill alone

to make something out of your broken home,

to work hard just so your daughters can have something
to look at.

Mother.

I know that you had nothing to look at,

that you dug inside of your own bones

to find the materials to make us whole.

For Girls Who Become Women

That you gave us all you got.

I will never not call you artist,

never not be in awe of what you created out of dust and
wanting better for us;

will never not think that you deserve every bouquet that
I can get my hands on.

For the words you gave me courage to write,

for the tears that you have wiped,

In every stage of living this book.

For being living proof

that you can always start again

-for being my first,

And dearest friend.

I love you. May you never doubt it.

'My yellow rose,

Wasn't always perfect

....

But I'd pick you every time.

WHENEVER YOU FEEL ALONE IN THIS LIFE THING,
JUST START BREATHING
JUST KEEP REPEATING

" WE ARE ALL, MORE **ART**
THAN CRAZY."

~ JESSICA ALYSE

Jessica Alyse is a heart searching, truth telling – poet.
While she possesses an unwavering love for writing, she
strongly believes that it is a God given vessel used solely to
connect with others – that all people desire to feel
understood and that when we begin to tell our truths, we
meet in the middle. She accredits the honing of her craft to
Howard University, where she was immersed in creative
freedom and liberal thought. If not writing, she can be
found admiring white carnations, over-analyzing
behaviors, or feeding into her stubborn inclination –
of trying to make sense of the heart.

~ about the author

Made in the USA
Middletown, DE
17 June 2019